FOREWORD

Here at Young Writers, we love to let imaginations run wild and creativity go crazy. Our aim is to encourage young people to get their creative juices flowing and put pen to paper. Each competition is tailored to the relevant age group, hopefully giving each pupil the inspiration and incentive to create their own piece of creative writing, whether it's a poem or a short story. By allowing them to see their own work in print, we know their confidence and love for the written word will grow.

For our latest competition Poetry Wonderland, we invited primary school pupils to create wild and wonderful poems on any topic they liked – the only limits were the limits of their imagination! Using poetry as their magic wand, these young poets have conjured up worlds, creatures and situations that will amaze and astound or scare and startle! Using a variety of poetic forms of their own choosing, they have allowed us to get a glimpse into their vivid imaginations. We hope you enjoy wandering through the wonders of this book as much as we have.

CONTENTS

The Poems

Toy Land

I could see a brilliant path made of Lego bricks
and trees made out of cotton candy.

I could smell gingerbread, sweets and chocolate
all at the same time.

I felt sticky honey and bumpy Lego bricks
and the grass swaying at my feet.

It could break my heart apart!

I could smell lollipops, white chocolate
and strawberries, it was amazing!

I heard birds tweeting, the wind blowing
and owls hooting in the pitch-black night.

I felt the wind pushing on my face
and I also felt the boiling sun on my back.

I felt like I was in heaven.

Ben Wells (8)
Bassingham Primary School, Bassingham

The Magic Faraway Tree

Inspired by The Faraway Tree

I could see a marvellous sight,
It stood there like adventures
Waiting to come.

I could hear the trees around
The magic Faraway Tree
Whispering to each other.

I could taste the sweet air
As a gentle breeze blew by.
I felt like I was in a different world.

I could see little doors and windows,
I could hear the little chattering
Of the little folk from the tree.
I could taste yummy cherries from the tree,
I could feel an adventure coming on...

Mya Makwana (9)
Bassingham Primary School, Bassingham

The Narnia Adventure

When you walk into Narnia,
the animals are really scared,
You see the tree and the door
that is the home to an elf,
You can hear the gentle purr
of the snow leopard,
The fumes of the tea from the pub
brings a smile to your face.

The bouncing of a mushroom
brings a cold, snowy touch,
The taste of freedom is lovely,
The look of the queen's castle
brings a shiver to your skin,
With the shriek of the elf
it's a lovely place.

Joe Cooper (8)
Bassingham Primary School, Bassingham

Lazyland

In Lazyland, where everybody is lazy,
Nobody needs to pay taxes.
All they do is stay around all day,
No farms, no need for much hay.

In Lazyland, there are no clubs,
Not even Beavers, Scouts or Cubs!
You even see them sunbathe on the toilet,
They can't be bothered to keep the door shut.

In Lazyland, all they eat is chocolate.
All they do is lie around in their huts.
Everything would be so boring to us,
Nobody even drives a bus.

Jimmy Gowrley (8)
Bassingham Primary School, Bassingham

Candy Land

I can see chocolate tree trunks
With green icing leaves,
Apple pencils on the ground
And cotton candy in the sky.
I hear birds tweeting loudly,
Musical bells and flowers are singing.
I feel really happy with candy all around me.

I taste sour and sweet and sweet candy,
Some are yucky!
I smell the fresh, strawberry air,
I feel biscuit crumbs beneath the grass like mud,
I touch blue sprinkles like the rain.

Carys Hatfield (8)
Bassingham Primary School, Bassingham

A Crash In Doughnut World

There was an alien who saw space in his rocket
Then his spaceship lost control and he was scared
The ship crashed into the sweet-scented
Doughnut World
He fell headfirst into the delicious batter.

The alien felt sad and lost until a dragon came
The dragon helped the alien make friends
When it was finished, the alien hopped back in
And went to space with a grumbling roar.
Then he made yummy-smelling cookies.

Amelia Oxby (8)
Bassingham Primary School, Bassingham

A Magical Journey

I see a land so dark and dull
Something is standing right behind me.
I feel very scared and am still as it steps closer
I hear a heavy whistle of the wind through my ears.
I taste the smell of a warm burning,
Should I have a look?

Now I see a hall of food gleaming right at me
I hear lovely music filling up my cold ears
I now look back and taste something like the forbidden fruit
I now feel like an explorer.

Amber Rose Chambers (8)
Bassingham Primary School, Bassingham

Up, Up, Up And Away To Graffie Land

I saw a flying graffie
It was making a hideous, snorting noise,
I felt the graffie's wings beating the air down,
Inside, I felt happiness, freedom and peace.

I saw a baby graffie sitting on the ground
waiting for her mother,
I heard them talking to each other in loving tones
I felt the echo of the low, snorting noises
in the background,
Inside, I felt special in Graffie World.

Beatrix Aurora Marti (8)
Bassingham Primary School, Bassingham

The Candy Hotel

I see a yummy, delicious land right behind me,
I hear loud noises clattering behind the door,
I smell chocolate on the door,
I touch candyfloss grass outside,
I feel really happy that candy is all around me.

I see a table with all kinds of sweets on it,
I hear the pops of popping candy everywhere.
I smell sweets wherever I step,
I touch giant lollipops.

Isabel Dorey (8)
Bassingham Primary School, Bassingham

Sweet Land

I can hear the milk ocean running through
my brain
I can see the wafer castle while I'm in my boat
Inside, I can feel the shiny crown
I can touch the metal gold.

I can smell the outside of the castle
I can taste sweets and the chocolatey drip
I can see the candyfloss clouds in the sky
I can feel the popping candy popping in my mouth.

Chelsey Amelia-Mai Conroy (8)
Bassingham Primary School, Bassingham

Sweets

Gums are great because they are sweet,
Gummy bears are sweet like apples,
Chocolate is the best,
I love pick 'n' mix because they are the nicest.

Lollies are lolly-like and I love them so much.
Jam is chewy because it is sticky and pink,
Jelly beans are tasty,
Marshmallows are white, they are amazing.

Amelia Walker (8)
Bassingham Primary School, Bassingham

Candy Land!

The dazzling candyfloss clouds shine brightly,
You can taste the sour lollipop,
You can smell the doughnuts,
You can hear the crunching chocolate bar.

You can see the burger Saturn,
You can taste the chocolate cookies,
You can smell the candy canes,
You can hear the cracking fireworks, *boom! Boom!*

Amelia Rose Firth-Garland (8)
Bassingham Primary School, Bassingham

Cookies

My bunny is called Cookie,
But I wouldn't want to eat him!
I would prefer delicious, tasty chocolate
chip cookies,
They smell scrumptious and chocolatey.

Soft chocolate melts in my mouth,
I can hear them calling from the cupboard,
I love chocolate chip cookies,
But I love my bunny, Cookie, best.

George Alexander Slater (8)
Bassingham Primary School, Bassingham

Skeleton House

Bony skeletons were wandering about
The terrifying house,
Creaking, loud noises,
Cobwebs tangling over my thick bones,
I'm happy being a skeleton.

The house was extremely huge,
Smell the coldness in the air.
Banging noises are coming from the skeleton gym,
I'm hoping to develop some muscle!

Tom Mathias (8)
Bassingham Primary School, Bassingham

Sweety Fun Land

I can smell the smell of the scrumptious lollipops,
I can see the cocoa river,
I can feel the sweet chocolate bridge,
I can taste the sweet, tasty lollipop,
It makes me feel like a flowing chocolate river.

I can hear the birds sing,
I can see the chocolate pot bubbling,
It makes me feel special.

Emily Hunt (8)

Bassingham Primary School, Bassingham

Steam Train World

I love this train journey, but it makes me feel weird,
I hear every sound like the wheels of the train,
I taste the cold air from outside,
I smell the steam from the train.

I see the seat in front of me on the train,
I feel the comfy seats,
I hear the engine roar,
I can touch the cold window.

Edward Schofield (8)
Bassingham Primary School, Bassingham

Candy Land

The candyfloss clouds shine in the sunlight
You can hear the silent gusts of wind in the distance
You can smell the sweetest of smells
I'm so excited.

You can see so many things to eat
You can smell the mint candy canes
Everything tastes so sweet
I feel like I'm floating on a cloud.

Charlotte McCracken (8)
Bassingham Primary School, Bassingham

Crazy Football Land

There are holes in the goals,
Hear the crowd cheer,
Burgers and hot dogs smell so yummy,
Nervous and excited about a win.

Go for a goal and I'm now whole,
Ends two-nil, but I still love football.
Now we've won, I've gone.
Now we've had a win, I'm up for a gin!

Josh Smith (8)
Bassingham Primary School, Bassingham

The Friendly Goblin

Birds flying high,
Juice from the friendly goblin,
Candy canes falling from the tree,
The butterflies whizzing around in excitement in your tummy.

Bunnies jumping around,
The slurps of juice,
The toadstools are sweet,
The butterflies settle down as the poem comes to an end.

Amelia Josie Jane Templeton (8)
Bassingham Primary School, Bassingham

The Alien Rat Race

The alien wakes up
Has breakfast
Washes
And sleeps.

The alien wakes up
Has lunch
Goes to work
And sleeps.

The alien wakes up
Has dinner
Sees his friend
And sleeps.

The alien wakes up
And sleeps
And sleeps
And sleeps.

Faye Willcox (8)
Bassingham Primary School, Bassingham

Scrumdiddlyumptious Land Of Delight

The pond feels thick and creamy,
The dragon smells candy wherever it goes
The waterfall was really quiet
Compared to the birds,
The dragon can see everything.

Franky the dragon sleeps,
He wakes up
And sleeps
And just sleeps, dreaming of treasure.

Miren Canale (8)
Bassingham Primary School, Bassingham

The Haunted House

One spooky night,
In a scary-looking house,
Two skeletons started working out,
They were best friends.

They wanted to grow fat,
They worked out every day,
They ate sardines, ham sandwiches and cake.
But the skeletons were still skinny!

Freddie John Gerald Hilton (8)
Bassingham Primary School, Bassingham

Burger World

Burger World is a fun place
If you want a sweet, yummy snack.
It smells of beef
And makes my tummy rumble

I'm feeling hungry
Brilliant, they're free!
Ten burgers for my sister and me,
Oh no! I feel stuffed!

Lily Conroy (8)
Bassingham Primary School, Bassingham

Moon Trip

I can see enormous holes in the ground
The spacecraft hums in the air
It feels like hard rock
Not soft cheese
I feel moony.

I set up my tent,
Loud music invaded it,
I felt a tremble.
The moon rocks.

Joseph David Eyre (8)
Bassingham Primary School, Bassingham

Candy Land

I can smell the candy here
A land full of fun
I can see the candy clouds
Dancing in the sun.

I can feel the candy grass
Tingling on my feet
I can taste the candy wind
I wonder who I'll meet.

Sophia Ann Slater (8)
Bassingham Primary School, Bassingham

Candy Land

C louds are like candyfloss
A eros are my teacher's favourite
N aughty is how I feel when I have lots
D addy doesn't like sweets, they make him fat!
Y ou will love Candy Land!

Fenn Morris (8)
Bassingham Primary School, Bassingham

Chocolate Land

The planet was tasty
It was warm
The place was scrumptious
The clouds were candyfloss.

The planet was chocolatey
It was lonely
The place was lumpy
The ring was chocolate sauce.

Callum Harrison (8)
Bassingham Primary School, Bassingham

Evil Burger

Bye burger bun, I'm up and running,
Come on guys, let's bounce to the skies!
The bouncy burger's just there!
Let's bounce in the air.
Let's bounce!

The magical fantasy,
Burger Land, we're here!
I'm off and I see cheese,
Let's run off and eat and repeat!

But, as I eat, my feet tumble
Upon a flying carpet made of cheese!
Crawling across the carpet,
I saw it took me to the stepping stones
But I needed to zigzag.

I'm hungry, let's get a burger.
The burger place was full of burgers,
There were no crackling crackers or pink piranhas
I walked and talked until I saw cheese sticks
I flew off and landed in a burger house

It was burned, I looked behind me
And saw a burned burger which was dangerous.
Another burger came
And squirted sauce at the burned burger.

Kian James Wright (8)

Beacon Primary Academy, Skegness

Rainbow World

If all the world were rainbows,
I would slide down a giant, magical rainbow
And land on the soft, fluffy cloud
At the bottom.

If all the world were rainbows,
I would slide down a warm rainbow waterfall
As warm as a hot, sunny day.

If all the world were rainbows,
I would swing on the magical, rainbow vines
In the dangerous rainbow forest.

If all the world were rainbows,
I would be edging across the rainbow cliff.

If all the world were rainbows,
I would slide down the rainbow
And find all the rainbow gold
At the bottom.

If all the world were rainbows,
I would be tiptoeing past
A beautiful rainbow unicorn.

Taylor-Jane Denny (8)
Beacon Primary Academy, Skegness

Magnificent Slime Land

If all the world were slime,
I would slide down the slippery, slimy fountains
I would play slime fight with my friends
And swim in the lovely, cool, blue slime.

If all the world were slime,
I would go to a slime park and play fun games
I would get lots of pink and white slime money
I would watch the birds swooping
In the wobbly sky.

If all the world were slime,
I would be tiptoeing past a scary brown bear
With jiggly eyes,
I would be swinging on a rope of slime.

If all the world were slime,
I would balance on a unicorn's slimy back
I would sneak past a slimy whale in the slimy sea.

Sophie Housley (9)
Beacon Primary Academy, Skegness

Candy World

If all the world was candy,
I would be sliding down a giant candy cane
If all the world was candy,
I would be tiptoeing past a liquorice, velvet lion,
If all the world was candy,
I would be walking across a bridge of cookie.
Crack! Crack! Crack!
If all the world was candy,
I would be still like a chocolate flamingo in a chocolate river.
If all the world was candy,
My foot would be tangled in red velvet
liquorice vines.
If all the world was candy,
I'd slip on a chocolate puddle head first.
Oh what a day!
If all the world was candy,
I would be asleep in a liquorice monster's mouth!

Charlotte Ann Greig (8)
Beacon Primary Academy, Skegness

iPad World

On a spiderweb, jumping on iPads
were two tall people.
They swung on cables,
clinging to the tall building.
As crunchy as cookies,
they went across the electric river
before the iPad monster came.
They used their cables to get across
but it was too late,
the monster had arrived,
they could not escape.
They saw a ruby case
so they jumped off the raft
and they swung on their cables.
Before they could get any further,
they were gobbled up!
They were breaking on the bones
but they kept on falling.
They never escaped.

Lewis James Flint (9)
Beacon Primary Academy, Skegness

Bubblegum Planet

In outer space
A planet so far away
Space is as black as liquorice
I have finally landed on a mysterious planet
What is this place?

I stepped onto the strange planet
It was very sticky
What was that?
It looked like a bubblegum alien!
I asked the alien what his name was
And he said his name was Bob.

I played some games with Bob
Then I had to go home
Because it was nearly midnight.
I had to say goodnight to the bubblegum planet
But I hoped I could visit the planet again soon.

Evie May Baker (8)
Beacon Primary Academy, Skegness

Autumn Food And Time

Getting lost in a marshmallow
Swinging on mud-brown gum
Crawling on a gummy acorn
Jumping onto a white, sparkly sugar-flake.

As jiggly as a jellyfish sliding down a ruler
Sliding down a pole
Falling down a chocolate banana.

Falling down a rabbit hole
Getting lost in earthy mud
As damp as dry slime
Clinging onto a cord.

Falling down a fluffy acorn
Geting lost in a cave
Crawling to be safe
As bouncy as a marshmallow...
Here I go!

Sophie Morrison (8)
Beacon Primary Academy, Skegness

The Magical Candyland

Getting lost inside a candyfloss maze,
What is that up ahead?
I finally found my way out of the maze.

Sliding down nice, warm, melted chocolate,
I made it down to the bottom of the chocolate.

What is that? Is that an ice cream mountain?
Yum! Is that chocolate ice cream?
Brr! It's cold!

Tiptoeing past a sleeping sweetie lion,
The lion's eye opened and I ran out.
I jumped and I got out
And crawled on a long Airhead.

Kelsie-Leigh Dunn (8)
Beacon Primary Academy, Skegness

Weird Wonderland

When I curled up in a ball,
I clung onto a white, snowy bunny.
I landed with a big thump on a block of honey,
Everyone thought it was funny.

When I curled up in a ball,
The bunny was hopping onto the ice
The water was made from cold-hearted ice
There was a giant, frozen dice
On the end of the ice.

When I curled up in a ball,
All of this happened.
But, then I woke up
On a treetop!
Oh what a weird dream that was.

Bella Cooper (8)
Beacon Primary Academy, Skegness

If The World Was Covered In Paper

If the world was covered in paper,
I would wrap myself in bubble wrap
And have paper to gobble it up in one go
And have a trampoline to bounce on.

If the world was covered in paper,
I would have a paper friend to play with
And I would make real people:
Dolphins, whales, sharks and fish.

If the world was covered in paper,
I would have a pet paper fish
And I would cover myself in paper
And fly to space.

Faith Amelia Rhodes (8)
Beacon Primary Academy, Skegness

Dragon World

If all the world had dragons,
I'd fly on them and help people
I might even fly to the moon!

If all the world had dragons,
I'd train them to breathe fire and save the day.
I could even make some breathe water
So they could go underwater.

If all the world had dragons,
I'd find sunken submarines and ships
I'd even train them to eat things from the ground.

David Spowage (8)
Beacon Primary Academy, Skegness

The Burger World And Different Stuff

One day in Burger World,
(A normal world, totally!)
We were having a nice sing-song,
And this is what it was:
Falling into a pit of doom,
I landed in a great big room.
(Best song ever, totally!)
The room was as crunchy as a biscuit,
As safe as a house,
As tough as a fort.
How could we get out?
We'd have to eat our way.
(Best plan ever? Totally!)

Jake Parkins (8)
Beacon Primary Academy, Skegness

Candy World

If all the world were candy,
I would eat the cats
And love the dogs.

If all the world were candy,
I would swing on liquorice
And never leave Candy Land.

If all the world were candy,
I would climb on cookies,
I would crawl across a KitKat.

If all the world were candy,
I would slide down chocolate,
I would jump on marshmallows.

Peyton Amelia Holyer (8)
Beacon Primary Academy, Skegness

The Land Of Maths

As wormy as subtraction spaghetti under your bed
As sheltered as a silky maths marshmallow bed.
As young as gloomy numbers very cold indeed,
Trapped in blocks of ice, solid, breeding raindrops.
The sun was coming up,
Melting the solid, icy block.
Finally being free,
Melting and melting,
Melting and it stopped.
I bashed the ice.

Jaylea Nowicki (8)
Beacon Primary Academy, Skegness

Scary Jungle

Imagine if there was a scary tree in the jungle
That looked like a crocodile.
Imagine if the ground was
As soft as pillows in the jungle.
Imagine if there was a puddle
Which was a swampy river in the jungle!
Imagine if there was a damp stick
That looked like a dead cricket in the jungle.

Corey Redfearn (8)
Beacon Primary Academy, Skegness

Candy Land

The chewy chocolate melts
like fluffy, pink ice cream
The lollipops are as hard as a pointy rock
The lollipops stand as proud as the prime minister.

The marshmallows are as soft
and as squishy as a trampoline.
The houses are made out of big bonbons
and chocolate lollipops.

Reshy Bains (8)
Beacon Primary Academy, Skegness

Mythical Creatures

Imagine a world of creatures
Flying and twisting in the air
Imagine things happening to you every day
I would have magical creatures in my world.
I would be flying on an alicorn each day
I wish I would come at Christmas
It would be such a treat!

Ella Brummitt (8)
Beacon Primary Academy, Skegness

Michael Falls Down The Hole!

Michael finds a rabbit hole
He goes in and finds a mole!
Michael finds a bottle, he drinks it
He then turns bigger bit by bit.
A rabbit appears to help,
Michael makes a yelp.
"Did you drink the magic bottle?" she says.
"Yes I did."
Then he goes to bed.
Michael then drinks something else,
He then turns back to himself.

Michael Warren Peacock (7)
Coomb Briggs Primary School, Immingham

Bunny Hop On The Top

Bunny hop, hopped on top of the moon.
Bunny hop, hopped on top of the top.
He flapped and fell and flopped
He found a house made of badges
He thought he was very lucky.
Bunny went inside
And met an alien called Toe,
He wore a suit and a bow,
They became friends
And went to Laice,
They ate a chocolate face.

Ella Coates (7)

Coomb Briggs Primary School, Immingham

Teaching Ice Cream Cones Karate

My ice cream students earning a golden belt
Hoping their cream will not melt.
They have some might,
I am willing to fight.
They are so good
They get a break with a chocolate flood.
I love them with all my heart,
We send them in a cart.
Ice cream cones, ice cream cones,
Oh you feel like foam!

Amelia Gilboy (7)
Coomb Briggs Primary School, Immingham

Cupcake In A House

A cupcake went into the house
It found and ate a little mouse
The cupcake wanted to bake
Then she wanted to decorate.
The cupcake went into the room,
She found a bristly broom.
The broom ran away
And the cupcake had a good day.

Darcey Pulford (7)
Coomb Briggs Primary School, Immingham

I Ride A Lightning Bolt

I rode a lightning bolt
It was not a bit of salt.
It had a shiny light
Which was very bright
It gave me a fright.
I went on a mission to the sea
Where the lions chewed,
The salt got them all
And they all had a ball!

Daniel Brown (8)
Coomb Briggs Primary School, Immingham

Scary Dragon

The dragon was big and long.
He had sharp teeth
And I ran down the stairs
I was very scared,
He had lots of fire and slime.
He kept chasing me all the time.
I ran as fast as I could
Into the deep, dark wood.

Issak Clarke Hargreaves (7)
Coomb Briggs Primary School, Immingham

Blue Monster

In Monster World, Blue was surfing in a black hole.
It was covered in gum like a bowl.
The next day, Blue went fishing for fish
And they ended up being cooked and in a dish.
Blue enjoyed the food
Which was good.

Elliot Carter (7)
Coomb Briggs Primary School, Immingham

On The Rainbow

I was sat on a rainbow as big as a snail,
It started to grow as big as a whale
Suddenly the colours shone so bright
That it looked white!
The rainbow was made out of popcorn
And I rode on a unicorn.

Lucyanne Sane Toure (7)
Coomb Briggs Primary School, Immingham

The Large Rocket

If you skip on a rocket,
Make sure you lock it.
Watch you don't tangle yourself,
You'll end up like an elf!
The rocket goes up in the sky
And it goes up to fly
And we say goodbye.

Gracie Groce (7)
Coomb Briggs Primary School, Immingham

Candy Land

I asked my mum,
"Can we go to the beach?"
"Yes of course, Leech."
The beach was made of candy,
It was fine and dandy.
There was a treasure chest,
It was the best.

Logan Robjohns (7)
Coomb Briggs Primary School, Immingham

Swim In A Cookie Sea

Joe went to Cookie Moon,
Up on a big balloon,
He wanted to go for a swim,
So he took Isaac with him.
They jumped into the cookie sea,
And ate lots of cookies, yummy!

Joe-Louis Smith (7)
Coomb Briggs Primary School, Immingham

Hot Dog Burger

The hot dog burger is smooth
And it can move
The hot dog burger can jiggle
And wiggle
The hot dog burger is slimy
And whiny
Oh, I do love a hot dog burger!

Cameron Watson (7)
Coomb Briggs Primary School, Immingham

The Cow

The cow likes to fly in the sunny sky,
He floats and floats up to the clouds so high,
From there, he gets a beautiful view.
He lies back on the clouds and moos.

Jace Crisdian Blakeman (7)
Coomb Briggs Primary School, Immingham

Space Rocks

Fry cheesy moon rocks,
They taste good,
You could eat them in the cheesy woods.
Fish off the moon,
You could get there in a hot-air balloon.

Freddie Hurley (7)

Coomb Briggs Primary School, Immingham

Barbecue

They were underwater with their fryer,
The cheese and moon rock which caught fire.
But then Earth shook up
And knocked over a cup!

Lily-May Maisie Gartland (7)
Coomb Briggs Primary School, Immingham

The Lonely Giant

The lonely giant had no home,
But, in the distance, he saw a dome.
It was made out of pie,
Which was high in the sky.

Elizabeth Mary Grills (7)
Coomb Briggs Primary School, Immingham

The Funny Zoo

The lion's fur was hot
And his food was in a pot
The kangaroo escaped from the zoo
And they found him on the loo.

Bailey Alexander Richardson (7)
Coomb Briggs Primary School, Immingham

Akinator The Genie

Inspired by Akinator

The genie is a guesser,
He reads people's minds
He's friendly and funny,
He cheats by going on his phone.

Jakob Gould-Love (7)

Coomb Briggs Primary School, Immingham

Things That You Find In Harry Potter's Hat

In Harry Potter's hat,
there was a hard-working, wonderful wand;
a bewitched, grumpy troll
and a spellbinding, big dragon
In a unicorn's horn, there was a silly,
scarlet-red parrot,
a friendly, white ghost
and an outstanding, gold charm
In a beehive, there was a magical,
white and silver pencil,
a flying, shiny motorbike
and an invisible cape that glows in the light
In a flying car's boot,
there was a magnificent, ginormous castle,
a sparkly, scary ghost
and a grumpy wizard's spellbook
In a witch's home, there was a green,
slimy wand, a very disgusting, little witch baby

and a secret, magical motorbike
in a dark, spooky garage.

Emily Butcher (7)
Ingoldsby Academy, Ingoldsby

Things You Find In A Wizard's Hat

In a wizard's hat, you will find
a wonderful Whomping Willow
and a menacing, parapsychological Dementor
and an eerie, miraculous motorbike.
In a wizard's hat, you will find
a mystical, bewitched broomstick,
an unusual, spooky wand
and a spiritualistic, petrifying owl
In a wizard's hat, you will find
a diabolical troll, a ghastly, ghostly gargoyle
and a petrifying, putrid dragon
In a wizard's hat, you will find
a marvellous Golden Snitch,
a magic, mystical phoenix
and a dangerous, deformed goblin.

Perry Ebbins (8)
Ingoldsby Academy, Ingoldsby

Things That You Find In A Wizard's Hat

In the mysterious hat, I saw
An enchanting, fascinating charm
A wonderful, uncanny wand
And a weird, haunted troll

In the mysterious hat, I saw
A weird, eerie Dementor,
A haunted, ghostly gargoyle
And a peckish, spooky Death Eater

In the mysterious hat, I saw
A haunted, bewitched broomstick
A witch-like, weird goblin
And a spooky, uncanny dragon

In the mysterious hat, I saw
A wizardly magic spell
A runic, witch-like castle
And an eerie, enchanted charm.

George Holland (7)
Ingoldsby Academy, Ingoldsby

Things You Will Find In A Wizard's Hat

In the majestic hat, I discovered
a fiendish dragon, a bewitched, ugly troll
and a weird Whomping Willow
In the mysterious hat, I found
an otherworldly, parapsychological Death Eater,
a wizardly ghost spell and a witch-like broomstick
In the magic hat, I found
a marvellously haunted Snitch,
a witcheting, enchanted cape
and a spooky, magical unicorn
In Ron's hat, I discovered
an enchanted motorbike,
a ghostly Dementor
and a spooky, witchly spell.

James Lenton (8)
Ingoldsby Academy, Ingoldsby

Things That You Find In Harry's Hat

In Harry's hat, I found
a gloomy, ghostly gargoyle,
a fiendish, jealous dragon
and a bewitched Dementor
In Harry's hat, I found
a jealous, parapsychological Death Eater,
a miraculous spell and a weird owl!
In Harry's hat, I found
an invisible cape, a weird, eerie broomstick
and a magical, spooky spell
In Harry's hat, I found
enchanted, mystical unicorn blood,
an enchanting parapsychological jewel
and an eerie, weird Whomping Willow.

Jesse Wells (8)
Ingoldsby Academy, Ingoldsby

Things That You Find In A Ghost's Hat

In the ghostly hat,
I saw a powerless but monstrous
necklace of anger,
demon dementor and
charming, spellbinding owl,
In the ghostly hat,
I saw an invisible cape flying in the sky
and an invisible owl,
In the ghostly hat,
I saw a dementor flying a motorbike in the sky
and a magical broomstick flying in the sky,
In the ghostly hat,
I saw a charming dragon
and a willow castle.

Estelle N (8)
Ingoldsby Academy, Ingoldsby

I'm In A Crazy Dream!

I'm in a dream right now,
But I can't wake up
And I don't know how!
I'm in a wonderland full of sweets and candy
You never know, they may come in handy.
Sweets, sweets and even more sweets,
Prancing around like music beats.
Snakes and ladders in the sky,
You can't really play them because they're so high.
A field full of bubbles that go *pop,*
If you want to get across, you might have to hop.
An underwater BBQ filled with lots of fun,
Have a massive hot dog or a bacon bun.
Dress up like kings and queens
Then later have some baked beans!
Take a nap on the cotton candy clouds
And watch the crazy crowds.
May your day be filled with yay
And have a bright and sunny day,
Do you think my poem is great?
Now, I'd better go, I don't want to be late.

Ruby Pickett (9)
Macaulay Primary Academy, Grimsby

Worrying William

Worrying William went up to his bed
With all sorts of horrible thoughts in his head.
He climbed the stairs slowly,
They creaked with each tread
And he entered his room,
Struck silent with dread.
He ran to his curtains
And closed them with fear
And peered under his bed
To see if the coast was clear.

He got up and suddenly cried,
"I'm sure I heard something outside!
What if aliens are landing their ship
Getting lost on their way to the tip?
They'll be out all night,
Making that noise until dawn
Dumping their rubbish all over our lawn.
Or an angry, old giant who's lost his door keys
Or maybe a king's army of robots?

Perhaps it's a big storm called Hurricane Hector,
That his power could rip up our
whole house from the planet?"

Frozen with fear, poor William couldn't sleep,
So he gathered his nerves to risk a peep.
Shaking and quaking, eyes open wide,
He crept to the window and looked outside...
But the garden was empty, all normal and calm
There was nothing out there
That could bring him harm,
No sign of the silly creatures he'd feared,
So William went back to bed
Without any horrible thoughts in his head.
Sleeping perfectly well, having left them behind,
He smiled at the things he thought in his mind.

Ruby Oxborough (9)
Macaulay Primary Academy, Grimsby

Sans The Extraordinary Skeleton

Inspired by Undertale

An extraordinary skeleton,
Shivers down your spine,
Chubby belly, slippers smelly,
Face is hard to find.
He'll turn your legs to jelly,
Though he sleeps on the job,
Has a tubby body,
Though he'll turn you into a frog.

Beat me?
Ha, you'll have to move faster
To get past my Gaster Blaster.
Try to hit me, oh look, you missed.
Make me mad and you'll be squished.

An extraordinary skeleton
Shivers down your spine.
He'll be your friend,
You'll get along perfectly well

Unless you anger him,
Then you'll be burning in hell.

I prefer ketchup to lime,
Mess with me and you'll have a bad time!
You're just a mouse because I'm a god right now
So now you must bow
To an extraordinary skeleton!

Jordan Lewis Okopskyj (11)

Macaulay Primary Academy, Grimsby

Fairy Teddy

Chelsea said to the big fairy teddy,
"What should we do today?"
Teddy said, "We should watch a film."
Chelsea said, "Do you want
To go on an adventure with me?"
The fairy teddy said, "Okay,
Let's have an adventure together."
They had lots of fun,
Then became really good friends forever.

They went to the beach to watch the sky
And the birds flying like aeroplanes.
Teddy said, "What should we do tomorrow?"
Chelsea said, "Why don't we go horse riding?"
Teddy said, "Yes, but I don't know
How to ride a horse."
Chelsea said, "Do not worry,
We will sort it out, okay?
You don't have to be scared."

Chelsea Rimmer (10)
Macaulay Primary Academy, Grimsby

What Is This?

What is this?
Oh, it's something you would not miss,
I fell into my teacup
Only to find this...
There was half day and half night,
There were dragons snoring
Rainbows squealing
Unicorns farting
And Smarties smarting.
But, that's not all!
There was a duck that was ten feet tall!
There were houses made of meat,
Don't take a seat
Because there are mice near your feet.
An owl took me out for tea,
I shouted, "I went home you see!"
I drank and fell back into the teacup
Only to find my mum clearing up!
So, I'm writing this and realising
That I am not a poet
And did not know it!

Shahnaz Anwari (10)
Macaulay Primary Academy, Grimsby

The Talking Tree

In the bright and colourful forest,
A strange tree approached me.
"It's a talking tree," I said.
Then I heard a slam,
There was a tiny door on the tree.
"What's the door for?" I asked
In a terrified voice. The tree replied,
Saying, "It's for the goslings."
"Wow!" I replied.
The tree smiled, you could see him
Disgusting, yellow teeth and,
When he moved his branches,
The ground shook like crazy!
I wish I was a dentist
So I could make his teeth sparkly.

Megan Baxter (9)
Macaulay Primary Academy, Grimsby

A Bibalub

Monsters and goblins roam our woods
But you know what roams in our shrubs?
It's a Bibalub,
With 100 eyes and a horn, plus a tub.
Walk into our garden and have a dig,
But don't be a pig.
A Bibalub won't approve,
It will make you want to move,
So be fair
And always stay out of a Bibalub's hair.
With a beautiful horn
A pink belly,
The feet feel like jelly.
You will want rid of this creature
A Bibalub will become your teacher.

Faith Louise Rose Carroll (10)
Macaulay Primary Academy, Grimsby

Crazy Hairdo Land

In Crazy Hairdo Land,
There was a lady with crazy hair
So she decided to not go to the fair.
She had sticky hair
And was too scared to go outside
And was actually too tired to lie
So she started feeling like she wanted to cry
So she baked a pie.
She finally decided to go to the hair salon
Whilst she was eating a melon.
There was a hurricane,
So she went to see Harry Kane
Her crazy hairdo was over
As she saw a four leaf clover.

Georgia Robertson (9)
Macaulay Primary Academy, Grimsby

Candy Land!

C herry bonbons for bushes and trees
A pricot sweets for the busy, little bees,
N asty lemons make your mouths cringe,
D ragonfruit dazzlers might make a long fringe
Y ellow Airheads fill your soul.

L ifesavers with a hole
A fter Eights are great,
N erds leave you in a state
D o you think this poem is great?

Chloe Christine Alison Marshall (9)
Macaulay Primary Academy, Grimsby

Candy Warrior

Goodie Goblin walked down the road
Goodie Goblin saw a toad
Goodie Goblin stopped to stare
But didn't know what was lurking there.

The gumdrop ghouls were ready to fight
Ready to attack with all their might
But Goodie Goblin was prepared
Brought his friends to give a great scare.

Candy Kingdom was now safe
From the gumdrop ghouls.

Stuart Lawson (10)
Macaulay Primary Academy, Grimsby

The Fish Monster

Once I had a goldfish
And his name was Jerry.
I fed and fed him every day
But it turned out, he grew bigger and bigger
And then he grew legs and arms.
Soon, he was the size of a mountain!
He ate all the buildings and then drank the ocean
He may have done all those bad things,
But he's still my favourite fish!

Deon Barraclough (10)
Macaulay Primary Academy, Grimsby

Puppy Trouble

There are Frenchies
There are Maltese
There are pugs
And many different breeds.

They love to run and play
And show their love in a special way.
They rely on humans for their feed,
My dog is called Floyd
And he is my special boy.

Hope Brown (10)
Macaulay Primary Academy, Grimsby

The BBQ

How good would life be
If you could have a BBQ
Under the sea?
Starfish, dolphins, sharks and crabs
Love the smell of Mummy's kebabs,
Chicken drumsticks are rather hot
With the sharks deciding if
They should eat it or not.

Harvey Reynolds (9)
Macaulay Primary Academy, Grimsby

The Wacky Underwater BBQ

Under the seabed,
BBQ hot like lava,
Fish like hamsters,
Sharks like dinosaurs,
The person has no scuba stuff,
The barbie is sizzling
The fish bones go to the dog,
The shark's fin gets eaten.

John Hudson (10)
Macaulay Primary Academy, Grimsby

Cheshire Cat

There was a Cheshire cat
In a black and white hat
He slept upside down
With a big, grumpy frown
I think he thinks he's a bat.

Maycie Ellis (7)
Macaulay Primary Academy, Grimsby

The Blitz

T error everywhere and people in despair
H ere is war, it's best to prepare,
E veryone has a gas mask when you're there.

B ombs everywhere, run away, not over there!
L et's go on a train, but not over there.
I n the world, there's danger and a big scare
T here is war and nothing to compare
Z *oom!* Spitfires everywhere.

Bomb! Bomb! Better beware, war is everywhere.

Hitler's hits make the Blitz

When people die, people cry and let out a big sigh.

Bradley Siddle (9)
Reynolds Academy, Cleethorpes

Marvellous Mammoths

To keep these creatures very clean,
All you need to do is be a little mean.
Just whip their legs and they will go
As fast as a falling domino.
Before you do that, listen here,
Make sure you set up a pool near.
Once your mammoth has had a bath,
Tell it a joke and make it laugh.
Now all the fun is over,
The thing to do is feed it a clover.
That will fill it up until tomorrow,
Don't be fooled if it starts to sorrow.
Bedtime is as 9.30
So check once more to make sure he isn't dirty.

Lola May Best (10)

Reynolds Academy, Cleethorpes

World War Two

W orld War Two was very crazy,
O dd things happened all the time,
R uined some of the buildings
L ots of people sadly lost their lives
D ays went by, but the war still went on.

W hile this was going on, people had to be evacuated
A lot of people hid in shelters
R esting people in hospital beds.

T rains leaving all the time
W ars are scary, they shouldn't happen
O ver and over, people were bombed.

Amelia London (9)
Reynolds Academy, Cleethorpes

The Blitz

T his war is mad, it makes me kind of sad
H ave I been dreaming all along? It seems like I have
E veryone is safe, so I believe in England more

B eds in the Anderson Shelter are super comfy
L oads of planes in the sky, they really do fly high.
I n the Anderson Shelter, it's really warm.
T he end has to be near, it started in 1939 and it's 1944
Z ooming past go the planes. *Bang! Bang!* go the bombs.

Owen Pearce (9)
Reynolds Academy, Cleethorpes

The Greeks

O lympics are where different events happen,
L ots of different events.
Y ou wouldn't win medals, you would win a leaf hat.
M en were only allowed to join the Olympics, no women were allowed.
P eople were allowed to watch.
I t is very different to our Olympics now.
C ars weren't there in the Grecian Times.
S o many people entered the Olympics, except women because they weren't allowed to join the Olympics.

Jack Money (8)
Reynolds Academy, Cleethorpes

Aphrodite The Greek Goddess Of Love!

Crash! Whack! Boom! Splash!
The sound of a giant crashing into the waves
The remainder of blood that begins to mix with the foam
Suddenly, a bloody, beautiful figure appears
I hear her say, "My name is Aphrodite."
The sound of beautifulness ringing in my ears
As the ocean hits the strong, slippery rocks
Closer and closer she comes,
The Greek Goddess of Love,
Born from the ocean,
Aphrodite.
Aphrodite.
Aphrodite.

Laylah Bensley (9)
Reynolds Academy, Cleethorpes

How To Look After A Mammoth!

Have you always wanted a mammoth for a pet?
If so, go buy a large fishing net.
A mammoth needs a good habitat
And its favourite food is a rabitat:
Those are animals like a rabbit
Yet, with a rather peculiar habit!
If, when feeding, they give you an alarm,
Don't put yourself in any harm.
If you are reading this for the first time,
I would go back and read the rhyme.

Deanna Taylor (10)
Reynolds Academy, Cleethorpes

Blackout

B ombs skim past the window
L oud sirens flying through my ear
A ll around are worried people
C ars drive slowly past to not be seen
K now to be quiet, but I want to cry
O n the windows is all black
U nited Kingdom under attack
T he sky as dark as the night.

Emily Louise Seaton-Norton (10)
Reynolds Academy, Cleethorpes

Fabulous Harvesting

H arvesting juicy fruits and vegetables
A lovely day to celebrate
R ed and yellow leaves falling off the trees
V egetables are so fabulous and they are so fresh
E veryone eats lots of healthy things
S eeds are growing from the ground
T ogether, eating lots of food.

Libby-Mae Coates (7)
Reynolds Academy, Cleethorpes

The Four Seasons

As Winter slides into the village,
He casts a spell covering the village with snow,
Like icing on a cake.
He slides on the road whilst covering it with ice.
The snow is like a blanket of fur, floating down
from the heavens,
The delicate snowflakes are dancing like ballerinas.
Spring is near.

As Spring bounces into the colourful countryside,
The bright daffodils decorating the fields.
Leaves are getting tickled in the gentle wind,
Baby lambs hopping over each other.
All the animals sprint in the field.
Summer is near.

As Summer strolls through the lazy village,
She casts a spell, making flowers burst out
with colour.
The leaves shimmer in all different shades
of green,
The sunflowers are waving at the sun.

Jack Alexander Freeman (10)
St George's Church Of England Primary School, Stamford

The Four Seasons

As Summer whispers to the sun,
Gasping to be sprinkled with fresh water,
She gracefully strolls to magically put the sun in the sky.
She is the queen of summer as she whispers to the animals.
Summer's elegant shoes tiptoe across the world,
Her feet kicks her resplendent hair.
Autumn is on its way.

As Autumn loses all its leaves, they twirl to
the ground,
All the animals go into hibernating.
Autumn is lonely like an artist spreading rich, fiery colours of orange and yellow and gold.
The obedient leaves fall like graceful ballerinas.
She strolls through the world, the animals
are asleep.
She whispers to the old, oak trees,
"Winter is on its way."

As Winter wraps the world in a blanket of snow,
She does it secretively but swiftly.

The stunning snowflakes are all over the excellent world,
While animals are hibernating,
Winter is the queen of ice.
Her hair is as white as snow,
Winter strolls through the woods
As she shouts to the wind, her black boots marching proudly through the snow.
Spring is on its way.

As Spring sings to all the flowers, she wakes up all the animals,
Putting a green blanket of grass all over the land.
She's got golden hair as bright as the sun,
All the leaves are coming back.
Spring whizzes past Winter, laughing,
She jumps as high as a kangaroo, all excited.
Summer is on its way.

Ella Marie Martin (10)

St George's Church Of England Primary School, Stamford

Wonderful Seasons!

As Autumn smoothly goes through the warm
countryside, a person smells the colourful flowers;
red, orange, yellow and gold.
She chatters to the wise apple tree,
The blowing leaves scatter all over the floor and
people pick them up
She gently waves goodbye to the trees,
She waves calmly to the trees while she leaves
the countryside.
Winter is on its way.

As Winter strides through the freezing-
cold countryside,
She is running because her legs are frozen,
She wants to get warm.
Soon, as she gets closer to a shed, she really wants
to get there fast.
As she is running, she can hear the snow crackling
as she runs on it.
She is a hard-footed girl, that's why it's crackling
What a frozen day.
Spring is on its way.

As Spring glides through the boring leaves of the trees gently in the countryside
Soon, you see magical leaves just falling
side by side.
It is a bit chilly, but not freezing,
it will be warm soon.
It is a little warm, but not like a boiling-hot oven.
Summer is on its way.

As Summer flows through the boiling-hot countryside, you are sitting there, sunbathing and having ice cream and ice lollies
It is just too hot,
You'd better be just lying down all day.
You just don't want to do anything,
There are people and children and pools to play in and have fun,
You play around a lot.

Elizabeth Smith (10)
St George's Church Of England Primary School, Stamford

The Four Seasons

As Spring bounds ecstatically through the lush fields,
He paints the glorious flowers in colours of coral, baby pink and sapphire.
As flowers wave to the cloud-dotted sky,
Lambs smile gleefully as they leap through the tickly grass,
As beautiful as the sunset, flowers swing this way and that.
Summer is on its way.

As Summer floats calmly along the soft,
golden beach,
He sings like an exquisite bird in song.
As the ocean tickles the sand playfully,
Crabs sidestep over it as silently and as elegantly as a swan.
Palm trees glide along, waiting to settle down for the night.
Autumn is near.

As Autumn plods cheerfully along the leafy path,
She twitters to the world to enrol itself in a patchwork quilt,

Elegantly, leaves twirl as they fall to the dense ground,
The trees are soldiers standing tall, supervising everyone who travels beneath.
Autumn secretively whispers her goodnights to all the exhausted creatures.
Winter is near.

As Winter trudges gloomily along the coal-black road,
He spreads his depression through every house and soul.
As trees cover themselves in thick, pure white blankets of snow,
They crack their icy fingers in the storm-like wind.
As he menacingly whispers his goodnights to all the freezing children,
They doze off into a never-ending sleep.
Spring is near.

Poppy Evans

St George's Church Of England Primary School, Stamford

The Seasons

As Summer squeals her hellos to the animals
Summer's feet patter on the ground silently,
Her ombre hair is kicked by her dainty feet,
Magical sparkles come from her path as the summer sun rises.
She wears a pair of rose gold sunglasses and a sky-blue dress
She is the queen of heat and parties.
Autumn is next to come...

Autumn is here!

As Autumn gently steps into the air, relaxing,
Her lips touch the trees,
Miraculously they lose their leaves,
Their leaves fall like helicopters drifting delicately,
Autumn colours the dying leaves blood-red, jack-o'-lantern orange and gold.
Anyone who hears all about Autumn is surprised by her.
Winter is next to come...

Winter is here!

As Winter tiptoes mutely,
She curtsies to the sky and snow falls
down gracefully
Her ivory hair is covered in snowflakes,
Spreading snow all over the world,
Her icy and alluring appearance make people
want Winter.
Spring is next to come...

Spring is here!

As Spring bounces into the world manically,
She touches everything she sees.
Her sun and joy brings new life
for lambs, cows, puppies and more.
She colours flowers the colours of rainbows,
Spring is a lead for the new year.
Summer is next to come...

Thalia Rollinson
St George's Church Of England Primary School, Stamford

The Four Seasons

Swift is Winter as he spreads wishes and magical snow across the barren lands
He is always whispering to the stubborn wind
He is resplendent and is as perilous as a polar bear
And as white as a glowing moon on a black sky,
Putting the world to sleep.
Spring is on its way.

Spring skips as she awakes the forest animals
Leaves bow gently to their queen.
Once a land cold and bitter is now warm and colourful as the fields of daisies.
Emerald clovers spread from hill to hill,
covering the land in a green silk quilt.
She puts all creatures into a deep sleep.
Summer is almost here.

Summer's bark-coloured hair brings life into the world
As she runs, trees' emerald leaves grow back into place on the bare branches.
Squirrels run along the forest paths and branches of the great oaks.

Warm is Summer's heat on a sunny day,
Summer talks to wise, old owls flying in the wind.
Autumn is here.

Autumn rushes past Summer as he paints the land with red, orange and yellow.
Autumn's hair is as yellow as a harvest moon on a summer night.
Autumn is as lively as an elfin child,
Animals bow to their prince,
Autumn is as swift as a barn owl
as he puts the trees to sleep.
The cycle starts again.

Oliver Daniel Sumpton (10)
St George's Church Of England Primary School, Stamford

The Four Seasons

As Winter shivers through the frozen earth,
She cackles with evilness in the sky,
She brings the cold to the world,
With a grin on her face as the animals snooze,
As fast as a cheetah, she makes it snow,
Thankfully Spring is on its way.

As Spring blooms up with excitement,
The flowers grow quickly,
All of the animals are awake,
Gathering up for the next hibernation,
Birds making nests in the trees,
Flowers standing up straight like soldiers,
Butterflies out with the bees,
Lambs galloping in the fields,
Summer is near.

As Summer travels through the heavens,
It gleams down at the land,
All the beaches are open now,
The sea, the shells and the sand,
The flowers salute the sun in the day,

Then sleep with it in the night,
Fields scattered with roses and daisies,
Oh what a beautiful sight,
Sadly, Autumn is near.

As Autumn sways through the breeze,
The leaves are turning orange,
All the trees are losing their leaves,
It's nearly hibernation time,
The first time in ages, the ground has had a drink,
The sun goes away more,
They are asleep,
Winter is near.

Ashton Rawden
St George's Church Of England Primary School, Stamford

The Four Seasons

As Spring glides above the forests,
Dropping down bits of confetti onto tower-like trees,
Like a spy, Spring looks at the fuzzy, pink world,
Spring jumps onto the crunchy, pleasant blossoms on the tough ground.
Spring is a bouncing trampoline full of energy.
Summer is on its way.

As Summer rises up, laziness spreads the earth.
Plants and trees yelp for rain,
Everything's dying, water is running out.
"Summer! Please stop!" says the enormous oceans,
Which are trapped in a see-through glass plate.
All animals waiting for the next season.
Autumn is on its way.

As Autumn strides down the sky,
A new fresh, seasonal breeze blows Summer away.
Everything screaming with laughter that all the leaves of the trees turn red, orange and brown
And fall onto the barren ground.

Suddenly, a snowflake falls on a red leaf.
Winter is on its way.

As Winter slides down a frosty road,
Dots of thick, white snowballs fall from the chalky, white clouds.
Snowmen fill the world,
Everyone's happy but some people enjoy all seasons and some don't.

Muhammad Shahbaaz Sarfaraz (10)
St George's Church Of England Primary School, Stamford

Four Seasons

Summer creeps in the dead of night,
Spreading her love and joy.
When the world wakes up,
She sprints quickly behind some trees
To survey them frolicking
In her glorious sunbeams.

Autumn dances through the glittering meadow,
She hums a little tune to herself
Like a hummingbird in the first light of day.
Silently, she tiptoes up the first oak tree
And whispers her soft goodnights,
She gently bangs on the bark
So the conkers begin to fall.

Winter slides into action on her ice-blue skates,
She tosses her magic snowballs
That explode in the sky,
Covering the earth in a cosy, white blanket of snow
She gently taps the trees three times,
They shake and wobble as icicles as sharp as elephants' tusks

Begin to form on the frozen branches.
Then she stealthily slips away.

Spring could never hide
She blasts her boombox to top volume,
Painting the world with rainbows and colour,
She zooms around on her skateboard.
Her glaring brush in her hand,
She scoops up her boombox,
Then crazily rides away.

Georgie Rose Gray (10)

St George's Church Of England Primary School, Stamford

The Four Seasons

As Summer leaps into action,
The beautiful sun pops through the clouds.
The sun winks with mischievous joy
He speaks with happiness as the flowers grow
He skips like an elegant, cheeky child
As the sun fades, the rolling moon sets in,
Autumn is on its way.

As Autumn strides over the cold countryside,
The leaves fall down like parachutes.
As the trees say goodbye to their leaves,
They trickle down to the stony path,
He walks down a path as the breeze blows by
When all the leaves have fallen off,
Winter is on its way.

Winter slides in with snow covering the land,
He is as bitter as an ice sculpture.
He walks by shivering in the white snow,
He smiles when he sees the snowmen,
His magical powers sprinkle the land with snow.

As the snow clears away,
Spring is on its way.

As Spring springs into the countryside,
He spreads the land with flowers.
He is as shiny as the sun,
He sends the sun to shine bright
He is bringing joy to the earth.
As the sun keeps shining,
Summer will be back.

Ben Ward (11)
St George's Church Of England Primary School, Stamford

The Four Seasons

Autumn steps quietly in the crisp countryside
Whispers goodnight to all the animals.
She covers the world in crumbly leaves
She says, "Good luck," to the wise oak trees.
The leaves are red, gold, yellow lava
dripping to the ground.
She picks glossy conkers in the wind's breeze.
Winter is coming.

Winter is here,
She creeps through the bitter, bleak snow,
She covers the world with feather-coloured snow.
She has seen the cosy, wooden hut
The smell of yummy food comes to her.
The miniature, orange lights wink at her.
Spring is coming.

Spring is here,
She jumps and twirls,
She is a colourful, bursting flower
starting new beginnings.
Stare at the rainbow in the diamond sky.

She wears a dress of flowers
Bees, butterflies fly around.
Summer is coming.

Summer is here,
Summer lazily walks to a sunbed,
She lays until the sun beams
She saunters to the shade.
The sky is plain as the sun shines.
The sand is like a blanket sizzling.
Autumn is coming.

Nikola Kowalczyk (10)
St George's Church Of England Primary School, Stamford

The Four Seasons...

As Winter silently creeps past
the old, Autumn breeze,
He cracks his icy fingers
in the soft, frosty wind,
He gradually whispers to the jet-black trees,
While his coal-covered hat stays
attached to his head,
"Spring is here."

As Spring zooms past Winter
with a cheeky grin on his face,
The fields stay scattered with rich daffodils,
A coat of clover cloaks the hills.
"I must pirouette and I must sing,
To see the beauty of Spring!
Summer is near."

As Summer glides down to the magnificent world,
He gathers his dear, devoted flowers
The sun is a cannonball of fire,
The bees are abuzz.

He is like an exquisite summer creature,
The sun stumbles as he spies on the majestic birds.
"Autumn is near."

As Autumn marches proudly past
the dear, devoted flowers,
He nods his head to let the irritating leaves fly,
"Fall is here!"
The air is cool,
Days are short, it's back to school.
"Winter is near."

Ben Robinson
St George's Church Of England Primary School, Stamford

Changing Seasons

As Autumn marches through the chilly, frosty countryside like an artist,
scattering luxurious, splendid colours:
amber, flaxen and gold,
He mutters to the shrewd, old oak trees. *Whoosh!*
The respectful leaves fall like light-footed angels,
poised to wave goodbye to the trees.

As Winter creeps through the snowy-white countryside like majestic polar bears sneakily stalking their prey,
He whispers gently, "Fall to the ground like angels falling from heaven."
They say goodbye to the clouds.

As Spring perks up the fresh, new grass,
Newborn spring lambs vigourously bloom.
The aromatic perfume of freshly cut grass,
Daffodils and tulips pirouette like ballerinas,
Swaying and dancing in the fields.

As Summer approaches, the sun shines brightly,
Lawnmowers munch their way through the grass,
chomp, chomp!

Barbecues sizzling in the sun, burgers and burgers calling to me,
They are consumed, gobbled up.
Yum! Yum!

Max Leuen Jackson (10)
St George's Church Of England Primary School, Stamford

Meet The Seasons

As Winter majestically strolls
across the bitter grass,
She spreads the blank snow into every corner,
It would be impossible to spot an albino rabbit.
She whispers to the snow like a teacher,
Encouraging them to plunge
down from their clouds.
Spring is coming...

As Spring joyfully skips across the lush grass,
She spreads the flowers like an artist spreading
paint across the canvas.
It is like a rainbow has fallen on the ground,
She calls the bees to pollinate the flowers, which
are soldiers saluting the sun.
Summer is coming...

As Summer hops onto his skateboard,
Rock music pours out of his 90's boombox,
The sun burns the emerald grass glades, turning
them a beige colour
Autumn is coming...

As Autumn sadly saunters through the
depressingly green grass,
He spreads the golden and crimson leaves across
the forest floor.
He asks the freezing wind to blow the leaves
across the country.
And the cycle restarts...

Jakub Michalowski
St George's Church Of England Primary School, Stamford

Four Seasons

As Winter slowly slides through the countryside,
She covers the ground with all her delight.
Winter is so beautiful.
She is like icing sugar filling the ground,
Snowflakes come down like feathers in the wind.
Spring is on its way.

Spring is here,
As Spring slowly slides through the countryside,
The flowers start to bloom in all their colours.
Spring is amazing.
She covers the ground with beautiful flowers,
She is like a diamond.
Summer is on its way.

Summer is here,
As Summer slides through the countryside,
She is so hot that you can't step on the floor.
She is like a diamond in the sky,
There are no clouds in sight.
Autumn is on its way.

Autumn is here,
As Autumn slides through the countryside,
She covers the ground with yellow and
orange leaves.
The wind cries through the trees,
She whispers goodbye to the leaves.
Winter is on its way.

Lily Mae Asker (10)
St George's Church Of England Primary School, Stamford

Spring, Summer, Winter

Spring skips like an elegant gazelle
She sings like an opera singer, singing at the top of her lungs.
Swiftly but silently, she scatters seeds on the moist, spring ground and helps them bloom,
Like the magnificent sun, she shines as brightly as Jesus.
Spring is a gorgeous ballerina.
Spring is here and joyful.

Summer runs through the warm, summery fields that are as beautiful as a bright, rosy-red tulip,
She chats with great happiness like God in his finest form.
Quickly but quietly, she cures illnesses and diseases with so much care.
Summer is a pretty girl, like Heaven in its
finest form.
Summer is here.

Winter strolls like a tiger, searching for its unlucky prey.
He mumbles with great sadness.

Swiftly but secretly, he sprinkles snowflakes on the bleak, crisp ground.
The man is as dark as Hell in its newest form.
Winter is such a miserable and glum man.
Winter is here and dull.

Oliver McIntyre
St George's Church Of England Primary School, Stamford

The Four Seasons!

Autumn comes in the whispering wind,
Animals are going into hibernation.
Leaves swill around like ballerinas,
Trees go bald with no leaves.
The leaves are in deep piles,
A squirrel scuttles across the ground.
Winter is near.

Winter comes with the slippery, white frost,
Trees' fingers crack in the icy wind.
People have lovely, warm hot chocolates,
Snow is white like polar bear's fur.
Snowflakes parachute to the ground,
Crunchy snow is everywhere.
Thankfully, Spring is nearby.

Spring is here with joy,
Flowers bloom in the golden sun,
Daisies, poppies, buttercups.
Happy smiles all day long,
The sun is an orange sunflower.
Summer is definitely near.

Summer is here with the warming sun,
The sun has got its hat on.
People enjoying lovely, cold ice lollies,
Sheep thank their farmer for shearing them.
It must end now that Autumn is coming.

Lillie Mae Bix (10)

St George's Church Of England Primary School, Stamford

The Four Seasons

As Summer saunters through the elegant countryside
She speaks to her flowers proudly and precisely,
She is like a teacher encouraging her exquisite flowers to grow with her inspiring voice
"Winter is on its way..."

As Winter cheekily slides
through the icy countryside,
He sprinkles sparkly snow
all over the naked trees,
warming them up
Mischievously, he scatters ice
on the untouched ground
"Spring is on its way..."

As Spring prances
through the gorgeous countryside
She zooms through the mythical forest
Flowers spring up to her
in her bad-mannered games
"Autumn is on her way..."

As Autumn plods through the bitter countryside,
She lazily strolls like a sloth
along the barren ground
She silently whispers
to the skyscraping trees, "Get ready."
Leaves cheekily fall like skydivers with parachutes.

Tobias Eason (11)
St George's Church Of England Primary School, Stamford

Seasons

As Summer strides through the baby blue sky
The scorching hot sun smiles down the turquoise,
azure, gentle sea.
Along the pale sand, as you stroll shells crackle in
your feet like a crab pinching you.
Prickly palm trees waving over you,
Clouds look like cotton wool balls striking around
the sky.

Autumn leaves are falling down in the swift wind
Leaves crowding around, giggling like
human beings.
It's a place full of happiness,
Swirly wind blowing rainbow leaves flying like
a butterfly,
Autumn is here.

Snow wraps around the trees like a scarf,
Trees shivering in the ice-cold.
Snowflakes falling down the deep sky,
Ice crystals shaking like crackly fingers.
Ice-topped, rocky, steep mountains.

The sky is like a blue blanket,
They smell like perfume on your soft skin.
Flowers bright like the striking sun,
Reflecting like the sun.

Harley Whitefield (11)

St George's Church Of England Primary School, Stamford

The Four Seasons

As Winter plods through the milky countryside,
She floats aimlessly
like a lost soul wandering around,
She mumbles moodily under her breath
As she trudges along the ground,
She scatters crispy snow over the world.
Spring is on its way...

As Spring jumps through the emerald-green
countryside, she giggles energetically to the
newborn lambs.
She wears a smile every day which lifts spirits.
Summer is on its way...

As Summer skips through the flower-decorated
countryside, she wanders
with her head in the clouds.
With a click of her fingers,
the sun comes out to play.
She is an angel, spreading love to the world.
Autumn is on its way...

As Autumn strides through the leaf-covered
countryside, she whispers goodnight

to the sleepy animals,
She nods to the colourful leaves
as they dance to the ground.
Winter is on its way...

Ruby Louise Howlett (10)

St George's Church Of England Primary School, Stamford

365 Days

As the spectacular Winter sweeps away the final, remaining evidence of Autumn,
Snowflakes as majestic as ballerinas repetitively dancing, giggle their way to the ground
forming a smooth blanket of thick snow.
When the excited children open up their curtains like gates to Candy Land,
they wonder upon heaven in its finest form.
The stunning and spectacular sights of Winter has only just given us a speck of its full power
There is more to await us in the future.

Next, Spring arises with a mighty breeze
and a breath-taking sight with several varieties of majestic flowers
towering over the spotty ladybirds.
The attractive river blazes through the emerald-green grass.

Oliver Szilagyi (11)
St George's Church Of England Primary School, Stamford

Autumn

Crimson, blood-red, orange leaves gracefully
gliding through the welcoming breeze,
Conkers cracking under the ragged boots of the
elderly park-keeper,
The leaves giggle as the wind plays
with each of them,
Rakes scraping the concrete path,
Warm mounds of fluorescent leaves keeping the
conkers warm, temperate in the freezing air.
Trees jiggling from side to side like they're in a
dance competition,
Violent winds bullying the school run
on a Monday morning.
Tornadoes of bursting flames
dodging the trees' fingers,
A parade of wind storming across the town while
mortals sleep sound.
Goodbye Autumn, 'til we meet again.

Finn Caines (11)

St George's Church Of England Primary School, Stamford

Meet The Two Seasons

As Autumn approaches,
The autumn queen is covering the whole world in blood-red, orange leaves.
She uses her magical, glowing star,
It looks like mountains of crunchy leaves.
The queen of the leaves,
As the violent wind plays with the leaves,
The leaves giggle as the children kick them into the air.
It looks like a bomb is exploding.
Winter is coming...

Winter is here and the snowflakes drop to the calm, cold ground.
As the ice king waves his magic wand,
Covering the whole world in magical and dangerous snow.
The snow is a mountainous, white blanket,
He makes the deadly icicles hang from houses.

Jayden Hannah (10)
St George's Church Of England Primary School, Stamford

The Amazing Race

As sweet and dreamy as Autumn,
The amazing fine-flowing leaves gently blow in the cool breeze.
The leaves parachute down into the peaceful, soft pile of leaves.
I just can't wait 'till winter.

As Winter wonderfully falls into the snowy ground like polar bear fur,
The snowflakes twinkle with happiness like stars.
I just can't wait until spring.

As Spring scuffles sneakily into the field,
Flowers jump out with pollen.
Bees hurry over to the thousands and thousands of beautiful white and yellow flowers.

Alfie Graham (10)
St George's Church Of England Primary School, Stamford

Meet The Two Incredible Seasons

As Spring leaps through the calm, mild land,
She lies on the tickly grass,
looking at the endless sky.
As the cuddly sheep run around
on the soft, dry ground,
She whispers to the sheep,
"Spring, it's finally here!"

As Winter slips across the slippery,
glimmering land,
She slips on through an exquisite,
white blanket of snow.
As the bitter snowflakes fall to the
unbreakable ground,
She whispers to the towering trees,
"Winter, it's finally here!"

Caitlyn Gregory (10)
St George's Church Of England Primary School, Stamford

Winter And Spring

As Winter glides through the countryside,
Majestically trickling snow like a piece of
white paper,
Winter leaping about, spreading soft snow
through the countryside,
Winter is a prancing prince,
Snow like a new carpet,
Spreading black ice.

Spring spinning about all over the countryside,
Spreading pleasant spirit all around,
Heart-warming people open the door to Spring,
Spring spreading colour all around town,
Trees growing, grass green, leaves about.

Olly Clarke (10)
St George's Church Of England Primary School, Stamford

The Wagon Rocket

Once I found a dragon,
It was a silly, tiny dragon.
I noticed it was in a wagon.
My dad is a scientist,
And he turned it into a rocket ship.
I said, "Thanks, Dad, you're a perfectionist!"
Me and the dragon flew into space
It worked! I said, "Let's have a race!"
"Good idea," the dragon said. "Let's touch the moon with our head!"
We went to the moon and found a Martian,
And then we saw her little bed.
The Martian talked to us
and we couldn't understand,
But all we heard is that it wanted to be
in a rock band.
We said, "Hello!" and quickly waved,
But she was shy and floated away.
We caught her up and asked her name,
Then she said, "Fay."

Me and the Martian became friends,
But now it's time to go away.

Francesca Shannon (9)
Stickney CE Primary School, Stickney

The Upset Monster

On my way to the shop,
I saw a monster
I saw a red monster
I saw a hungry, red monster
I saw an angry, hungry, red monster
I saw a sad, angry, hungry, red monster
I saw a big, sad, angry, hungry, red monster
I saw a blood-thirsty, big, sad, angry, hungry, red monster
And it was upset
It wanted some sweets,
So I gave it some.

Jasper Edney (8)
Stickney CE Primary School, Stickney

Little Dragon Sparks

Little dragon Sparks
Likes to play with bark
When he was born
He had a glittery golden horn
He wanted to go to the store
But he was very poor
Gleeful he is
He has a friend called Fiz
They go to the park
To find some bark
Sparks likes to eat meat
And tries not to tread on his feet!

Erin Waller (9)
Stickney CE Primary School, Stickney

On My Way To The Beach

On my way to the beach, I saw a gorilla
He was a massive gorilla
He was a scary, massive gorilla
He was a hairy, scary, massive gorilla
He was a big-teethed, hairy, scary, massive gorilla
He was a purple, big-teethed, hairy, scary, massive gorilla
And he kicked over my sandcastle!

Melody Shona Michelle Lee (9)
Stickney CE Primary School, Stickney

When I Went Skydiving

When I went skydiving, I saw a rabbit
It was a happy rabbit
It was a happy, flappy rabbit
It was a happy, flappy, smiley rabbit
It was a happy, flappy, smiley, fluffy, nice rabbit
It was a happy, flappy, smiley, fluffy, nice, adorable rabbit
And it wanted to skydive with me!

Ollie Jai Bradshaw (8)
Stickney CE Primary School, Stickney

Witch's Fingers

The witch's fingers are as sharp as a needle
The witch's hat is as big as a house
The witch's tummy is as fat as the sea
The witch's face is as scary as a tiger
The witch's belt is as black as the sky
The witch's feet are as big as the road.

Callum Peter Smith (8)
Stickney CE Primary School, Stickney

The Evil Tooth Fairy

His teeth hands are as sharp as a super
sharp spear
His tooth hat is as shiny as a diamond
Also, his evil shirt is as evil as a devil
His teeth earrings are as expensive as a PS4
Also, his tooth boots are as dirty as a pig
And then he was after my teeth!

Harvey Lee Hills (8)
Stickney CE Primary School, Stickney

My Friend

On my way home, I saw my friend
He wanted to play tig
He wanted to play tig and superheroes
He wanted to play tig, superheroes and Deadpool
He wanted to play tig, superheroes, Deadpool and building
I said, "Of course, come on!"

Jayden Toulson (8)
Stickney CE Primary School, Stickney

On My Way To School

On my way to school, I saw a dog
It was a fierce dog
It was a fierce, angry dog
It was a fierce, angry, cute dog
It was a fierce, angry, cute, tall dog
It was a fierce, angry, cute, tall, fat dog
And it wanted to eat me!

Alice Waterson (8)
Stickney CE Primary School, Stickney

The Zoo

On my way to the zoo,
I looked out of my car window
I saw a flying cow
It was flying through the sky
It was as big as a bus
It was as funny as a clown
It was as fast as an aeroplane
And it was chasing me!

Lydia Minards-Roome (8)
Stickney CE Primary School, Stickney

One Morning

One sunny morning,
I woke up on a cloud
I jumped off the cloud
And flew high into the sky
I soared with eagles and hawks
I hung onto the tail of a jumbo jet
And then I woke up
And it was just a dream!

Oliver William Bishop (8)

Stickney CE Primary School, Stickney

Play Hopscotch With A Giant

I like playing hopscotch with a giant
He's a big giant,
He has a big hat
He has a big nose
He has a big belly
He has big feet
He has big hands
And he's a big cheater
I never win.

Molly Rose Warby (8)
Stickney CE Primary School, Stickney

On My Way Home

On my way home,
I saw a cookie monster
It was a fat cookie monster
It was a hungry, fat cookie monster
It was a puzzled, hungry, fat cookie monster
And he wanted to eat cookies.

Matthew Dean Falby (8)
Stickney CE Primary School, Stickney

The Lancaster

On my way to the car
I saw a Lancaster
It was a loud Lancaster
It was a loud, big Lancaster
It was a loud, big, flying Lancaster
And it wanted me to fly it.

Kyle Benton (8)
Stickney CE Primary School, Stickney

Forest Fire

As you can hear with your clear ear,
The forest is on fire
The fire is powerful
The fire is a big, powerful fire
The fire is a light, big, powerful fire.

Alfie Smith Foulds (8)
Stickney CE Primary School, Stickney

Have A Dog As A Pet

I have a dog as my pet
I have a fierce dog
I have a fierce, strong dog
I have a fierce, strong, friendly dog
And he needs to go for a walk!

Kitty Esme Ridgewell (8)
Stickney CE Primary School, Stickney

Den In The Marvellous Milky Way

M arshmallow moon craters.
A s I'm jumping across the craters I see the earth
R acing around the Milky Way.
V irtual life comes true.
E lephants fly up. I lift one with my left hand.
L aughter fills my head as I think of the elephant
L ooking up at the Milky Way stars.
O h no! My hair is stuck in chocolate!
U nder the stars, a star falls into my mouth
S parkling stars shining in the moonlight.

M ore and more, the Milky Way goes on
I loved being there, but it is not over yet!
L ine up stars and let me see you shine!
K ing of the stars is here
Y uck, he's got a moustache.

W hat? How am I floating in thin air?
A way I went down to the marshmallow moon
craters
Y uck, I used milk chocolate to wash the
chocolate out!

Hannah King (10)
Wyberton Primary School, Wyberton

Banana Racing Car

B ig, yellow, banana racing car ready to race
A nd we go, go, go, racing on the strawberries
N ot again! One of my liquorice wheels goes rolling
A way! Down the hill it goes!
N ot again! I was at the bottom of the line
A nd there it was, my liquorice wheel! *Crash!*

R acing bananas is not fun after all,
A lthough I could try it again.
C *lunk, crash, clunk!* The car rolled along the road, elephants came flying through the screaming crowd like lightning bolts
I f I could, I would stop it all,
N othing prepared me for this.
G ot it! I was so close to the finish line.

C an't do it because a car is near me, it is Donald Trump
A t the strawberry lace finish line, I came second.
R ace to space will never happen...

Brooke Ellice Smalley (10)
Wyberton Primary School, Wyberton

In Halloween World

In Halloween World, where the sludge monsters lay
It is simply impossible to keep monsters at bay
So, I wander through to see what will await me.
A competition that only monsters do,
It's horrible to see:
A big, slimy, monster-infested
Bogey-picking competition!
I must admit, it was quite a sight,
I tripped on a stick and fell through,
Then all the monsters shouted, "Boo!"
I closed my eyes and covered my ears
To the bellowing sound of cheers.
I was then greeted by a fortune teller
And, by the way, her name was Stella.
She greeted me with a glass of slush,
It actually tasted quite lush.
Then they told me I'd drunk eyeballs and fingers!
Yuck!

Isabelle Paige Whiley (10)
Wyberton Primary School, Wyberton

The Chocolate Fair Explosion

Sweetness filled the air,
Fluffy candyfloss stuck to my feet
The racing roller coaster created out of chocolate
Got everyone with fear and delight.
It's soon my go and I saw the chocolate explosion
And it got me giddy inside.
I immediately placed my bum on the marshmallows.

Now there was no getting me off,
This was the best,
I quickly took some cookies from the sky
And ate them in one!
The diver said, "We're near the Milky Way!"
I grabbed it and ate it all!
We got back and they had to drag me
Out of the seat,
My butt was like a magnet to the seat!
Just then, it exploded!
No one ever left, they swam in chocolate forever.

Louie Bates (10)
Wyberton Primary School, Wyberton

Sugar Land

Sweeping unicorns, all sweet and fluffy
Dropping off bonbon babies,
No cry to be heard
All the bonbons gathered around the mother's cot.

Flavours pop and spring
Filling my mind with the sweetest dreams
Meringue clouds as fluffy as can be,
I couldn't believe it as I stood on a macaroon mountain.

Waves of Skittles flowed so naturally,
Swimming in a wonderland sensation.
I slid down cookie mansions,
Candyfloss trees, so cheeky they can be
Sticking in my hair,
Gummy snakes slithered around.

Ouch! Oh no, I fell over M&M rock,
Getting back up, sugary snow begins to fall.

Sophie Featherstone (10)
Wyberton Primary School, Wyberton

Dozing Dodgeball

Dazzling Maltesers filled my eyesight,
Over the top of the candyfloss hill,
Zigzagging my way, I saw my opponents,
In the field of dreams, we met.
Nelson was ahead of me,
God save me!

Dodgeball isn't my thing, help!
Ovel, his teammate, threw the first ball.
Gosh! It hit the rainbow shield
Exactly! That shield, how quickly it disappeared,
Bursting under my feet, popping candy did its job
And the sweetness filled my nose.
Later, we got back into the game,
Large balls finally eliminated us.

Jack Clayton (10)
Wyberton Primary School, Wyberton

Underwater Fair

U nder the deep blue ocean,
N erno was swimming in the blue ocean
D odgems were crashing
E lephants were dancing to the music
R oller coasters were racing
W altzers were spinning around
A roma of onions
T ime to dance!
E veryone was having fun,
R ibbons of seaweed tickled my toes.

F ish swam all around me,
A ll of the excitement of the fair was
I rresistible,
R oller coasters swirling around.

Chantelle Brinkley (10)
Wyberton Primary School, Wyberton

My Pet Dragon

M y pet dragon, greens and yellows,
Y our ears must shut when he bellows.

P lease run or he'll eat you,
E at you he will, you'll be dragon poo.
T ry to run, try to hide,

D on't be fooled, he isn't on your side.
R un, run, as fast as you can,
A s his bite is more painful than being hit with a frying pan!
G ruesome breath will suffocate your body,
O ne more chance to run away,
N ever touch my dragon!

Davey Ogle (11)
Wyberton Primary School, Wyberton

Frozen Time

F rozen in time is not very good,
R unning from nothing, running from fun,
O verall, not nice, no one to talk to.
Z ooming cars stopped like ice,
E veryone stopped like the mannequin challenge
N o sound I could hear in the distance.

T ime is my worst enemy,
I feel like someone is talking to me.
M y friend, I think I can hear,
E yes were blurring and a man came out of the
frozen fog.

Jake Barsby (11)
Wyberton Primary School, Wyberton

Unicorns In Space

Floating away,
Miles away from the place that I love,
All the way up here and a view from above.
Way around the Milky Way
With shimmer in my eyes,
How could I not see this angel in disguise?
Look over there, what's that fascinating creature?
Colours, colours, too many to count,
I couldn't look away,
It was like an amazing feature.
That beautiful mane, swishing through the air
How could I resist this beautiful hair?

Isabelle Bowern (10)
Wyberton Primary School, Wyberton

Deep In The Beast's Belly

Deep down inside,
I can't hide,
For I'm inside this beast.
Oh yes, I have been its feast.
But, don't worry,
I'm not in much of a hurry,
Just trying to think of a plan.
I could be a man
Or I could be Little Red Riding Hood,
Although, I wouldn't be as good.
I need to speed up my pace
As now, it's me and time in a race.
Bye! I'm going down,
I will see you later, on the ground.

India Upsall (11)
Wyberton Primary School, Wyberton

Chocolate Hot Tub

M agnificent wonders follow me
A s many people can't really see.
G reat, vast unicorns swimming in candy,
I n that case, oh! That's fancy,
C ome and unlock my world!

H ot chocolate steaming up
O n a floaty shaped like a cup.
T his tub is a wonder!

T hank you for this chocolate,
U nder this is, ugh, Boring World,
B ye for now!

Sofia Jankauskaite (11)
Wyberton Primary School, Wyberton

This Is The Life

I can run at supersonic speed,
No one's faster than me.
I have a pet shark,
It makes me say whee
Faster please!

Now I've gotten back,
I get my trident
For I am now the president.
Follow me.

Thousands of merpeople followed,
So I took them to a family of whales
And they all hugged.
The mermen were eaten
Because they were being babies,
But I still didn't know why?

Joel Norris (9)
Wyberton Primary School, Wyberton

Running On Lava

Magma moulds into the cracks of lava,
The river of ruby-red flame
Flickers through tunnels like funnels.
Quickly, my feet withstand the heat
As I run over the mountain river
Bubbles of lava popping,
My feet are hopping.

With my feet hopping,
The magma was popping
And rocks crashed with bedrock, bashing,
It was like they were mashing and moulding rock
Lava in an endless stretch, going for miles.

Oron Jack Simpson (11)
Wyberton Primary School, Wyberton

My Book I Ate For Tea

As I ate my book, it was a bit plain,
My mum thought it was good,
But I thought it was lame.
She said, "Eat it to get good knowledge,"
So I said, "Fine."
I needed to get into college.
I wanted to be smart
So I could get on the good chart.
It was a really thick book,
The back was made out of paper
And so was the front,
I couldn't cope
Because I had a really bad throat.

Daisie Barnes (10)
Wyberton Primary School, Wyberton

Confectionery Chaos

Strawberry lace grass
And chocolate bar cars,
Gingerbread houses
And bricks made of Mars.

Candyfloss clouds
And marshmallow chairs,
The sky rains sprinkles,
Toffee apples and pears.

Double Decker buses
And gummy bear berries,
Cola bottles
And fizzy red cherries.

Victoria sponge castles
And honeycomb bees,
Jelly bean plants
And chocolate stick trees.

Charlotte Posey (11)
Wyberton Primary School, Wyberton

The Golden Pick 'n' Mix

Money starts to bloom.
This knocks out my gloom,
The chocolate trunk starts to melt and stick,
It looks good enough to lick.
The golden branches shine,
As I drink my wine,
The aquamarine flowers fall
As the money starts to form on the tree so tall.
The money fell
So I rang the bell.
My servants went to collect the money,
Even though it wasn't sunny.
Now, let the cycle begin again.

Alexander Kay (10)
Wyberton Primary School, Wyberton

Tea Is Served

Here's the elf,
Coming through the door at full pelt,
Waiting for a big portion of tea
Until I ask, "Is there any for me?"
I bring the plate, I knew it was a mistake.
The jelly goes *wibble, wobble* as I bring it through
The next thing you know, the elf needs a poo!
Finally, it's come to an end,
The elf hops out of his highchair
With a cheeky face,
This was a disgrace!

Chloe Rachel Allitt (10)
Wyberton Primary School, Wyberton

Cows

C ows are everywhere
O w! Cows hurt me!
W e did it all day cow,
S illy cow.

R hyming cow
U p and running cow
L ight up cow
E at up the white cow.

T oilet cow
H urry up cow!
E ww cow...

W orld cow
O h cow,
R ing up the cow
L oose-toothed cow
D umb cow.

Keira Carol-Ann Hancock (9)
Wyberton Primary School, Wyberton

Candy Land

As I enter the sweet candy land
I gather rainbow candy in my hand.
Sweet, sugary aromas fill the air,
Sweet, sticky candy in my hair.
Gummy snakes slither around,
Walking gingerbread men dig up the ground.
When the gingerbread men found something round,
They'd found an M&Ms in the ground.
Candyfloss clouds fill the air,
As I came across a big, sticky bear.
I follow it to its lair.

Kacey Turvey (10)
Wyberton Primary School, Wyberton

Marshmallow Park

M arshmallow Park, fluffy rainbows that you can eat,
A m I dreaming? I think I am.
R ain that makes pear drop puddles
S tuffed with strawberry Skittles, wow!
H urry! Come and see this,
M altesers are dancing on the sides
A nd Coke with gummy burgers with a
L ong,
L ong line to wait for.
O h no!
W ho can help me?

Gracie-Sue Mabaja (10)
Wyberton Primary School, Wyberton

The Minotaur

The Minotaur I scrubbed,
The Minotaur I loved,
The Minotaur had vicious claws,
The Minotaur had sharp teeth in his jaws.
The Minotaur had massive hands,
He also liked to sing with bands.
He liked to breathe out fire,
But only when he was at the mire,
He lived in a raven cave
So he was very brave,
He liked to eat crunchy nuts,
But his favourite was butts!

Ashton Stubbs (10)
Wyberton Primary School, Wyberton

F1 Hot Dogs Racing On A Rainbow

H ot dogs zoom on the track at 400mph
O ver the earth
T hey speed around the corners at 250mph

D omino's pizzas spectate them
O n the rainbow with
G uards around it.

R acing on the track
A nd cars beside them
C rashing
I nto
N eon
G ates.

Leon De Roeck (10)
Wyberton Primary School, Wyberton

The Candy Pegasus

In my eyes, I saw a door,
I opened it and I began to see more.
Walking to it, I saw candy
And saw a pegasus called Randy.
I saw a candy tree,
Then I saw a tasty cup of tea.
I approached it, but then I saw a key,
I used it on the door
And it led to a rainbow sea
And I wondered where the pegasus could be,
The one who created the key.

Faith Ponton (9)
Wyberton Primary School, Wyberton

The Gross Goblin

G ross green colour,
O val-shaped stomach,
B eautiful on the tail,
L ively as a wild dog
I maginative as can be
N aughty like a badger.

M artian,
E xtraterrestrial
R evolting
M arvellous
A ngry
I gnorant
D isgusting.

Madeline Ray (9)
Wyberton Primary School, Wyberton

Wonderland

Weird and wacky,
Down the rabbit hole,
Teacups and tea,
Where everyone is crazy plus me.

Where the impossible is possible
And everything is possible,
Having tea with the maddest guy around.
The Mad Hatter's bonkers, it's absurd.

But you're forgetting,
Anything's possible in Wonderland!

Isabelle Fitzpatrick (10)
Wyberton Primary School, Wyberton

Alien Party

I made some friends with some aliens,
They invited me to their alien party.
I thought I might play my violin.
When I got there,
It was bare!
All of the aliens jumped up, "Boo!"
The boys were wearing a bowtie,
The girls wore luminescent dresses,
When it was done,
It hadn't been fun.

Chloe Goor (9)
Wyberton Primary School, Wyberton

The Rainbow Land

Dancing, laughter and music,
In the deep blue ocean,
Submarines floating,
Crabs, lobsters and clams swimming,
Oh how funny to see them dance!

Inside the glamorous ocean, there's a party,
Three hundred feet deep,
Hearing waves breaking
Everywhere shining
Seeing colours all around.

Leah Faunt (10)
Wyberton Primary School, Wyberton

I Live Inside A Giant Rainbow!

I live in a rainbow, it's so cool,
I also have a giant pool.
I appear anywhere that has rain and sun,
But when there's a thunderstorm, I've got to run!
Everywhere my rainbow goes,
I love watching all the shows.
I learn new things, I meet new folks,
I always ask for their favourite jokes.

Chloe May Oswin (10)
Wyberton Primary School, Wyberton

Surfing On Lava

A volcano has erupted
Lava is flowing around
I jump on my surfboard
It's a lava tsunami
It's bigger than ever
It erupts like TNT
It's scary
But it's cool.
I surf quickly,
But it gets bigger
And bigger
And
Hotter
Until I nearly fainted.

Oliver Hutson (9)
Wyberton Primary School, Wyberton

Climbing A Volcano

As I climbed the straw,
I started to feel a big, massive door.
I peeked my head inside,
Then came out with a massive surprise.
I lost all my hair
Because of a big, volcanic flare.
I came to the conclusion
I would lose all my fusion
And never come back again.

Emilia Stubbs (10)
Wyberton Primary School, Wyberton

BBQ Under The Sea

A family and their pets had a BBQ under the sea,
I wondered what I would be having for my tea.
I wonder if it will be fish for tea?
We all sat down, no one had a frown
And everyone had a smile.
Everyone could eat now,
Even if you were on a diet.

Jared Wiltshire (10)
Wyberton Primary School, Wyberton

Young Writers Information

We hope you have enjoyed reading this book – and that you will continue to in the coming years.

If you're a young writer who enjoys reading and creative writing, or the parent of an enthusiastic poet or story writer, do visit our website **www.youngwriters.co.uk**. Here you will find free competitions, workshops and games, as well as recommended reads, a poetry glossary and our blog. There's lots to keep budding writers motivated to write!

If you would like to order further copies of this book, or any of our other titles, then please give us a call or visit **www.youngwriters.co.uk**.

Young Writers
Remus House
Coltsfoot Drive
Peterborough
PE2 9BF
(01733) 890066
info@youngwriters.co.uk

Join in the conversation!
Tips, news, giveaways and much more!

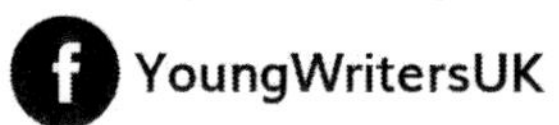